21st-Century
Engineering Solutions
for Climate Change

AIR QUALITY AND POLLUTION

KAITLYN DULING

Cavendish
Square

New York

Published in 2019 by Cavendish Square Publishing, LLC
243 5th Avenue, Suite 136, New York, NY 10016

Copyright © 2019 by Cavendish Square Publishing, LLC

First Edition

Library of Congress Cataloging-in-Publication Data

Names: Duling, Kaitlyn, author.
Title: Air quality and pollution / Kaitlyn Duling.
Description: First edition. | New York : Cavendish Square, 2019. |
Series: 21st-century engineering solutions for climate change |
Includes bibliographical references and index.
Identifiers: LCCN 2017054203 (print) | LCCN 2017055908 (ebook) |
ISBN 9781502638434 (ebook) | ISBN 9781502638410 (library bound) |
ISBN 9781502638427 (pbk.)
Subjects: LCSH: Air--Pollution--Juvenile literature.
Classification: LCC TD883.13 (ebook) | LCC TD883.13 .D85 2019 (print) |
DDC 628.5/3--dc23
LC record available at https://lccn.loc.gov/2017054203

Editorial Director: David McNamara
Editor: Kristen Susienka
Copy Editor: Rebecca Rohan
Associate Art Director: Amy Greenan
Designer: Megan Mette
Production Coordinator: Karol Szymczuk
Photo Research: J8 Media

Printed in the United States of America

CONTENTS

CHAPTER ONE

THE AIR OUT THERE

Take a moment, close your eyes, and take a deep breath. Feel your lungs fill with air. Maybe you are sitting inside and you smell a meal cooking in the kitchen, or the laundry that desperately needs to be washed. Or perhaps you're outside and the scent of freshly cut grass or clean snow fills your nose. Do you cough? Is it hard to catch your breath? Now slowly let the air out, back into the space around you. Feel your shoulders relax. Look up, and look around.

Opposite: This dandelion's seeds escape into the air.

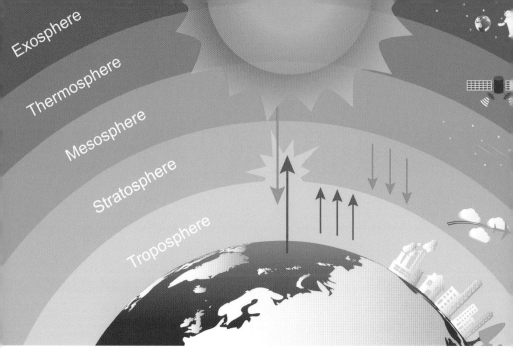

This diagram shows the different layers of our atmosphere.

Why Care About Air?

How often do you think about the air around you? You use it every single day. In fact, you use it every second of every day! Our bodies need clean air in order to function properly. While our bodies are built to handle all kinds of things in the air, they aren't indestructible. When the air isn't clean, it can have physical ramifications for our bodies and even bigger, more far-reaching and devastating outcomes for the world around us. The quality of the air is impacted by countless sources—transportation, industries, natural disasters such as forest fires, agriculture, and so much more! However, it's not just the air outside that can be affected. Indoor air pollution—that is, the introduction of substances that can have harmful effects—exists in schools, businesses, and homes around the world. Each day, we take over twenty thousand breaths. You may not notice it, but over 3,400 gallons (12,870 liters) of air are moved in and out of your lungs during the day. That's a lot of air, especially if it's polluted. Polluted air doesn't just affect our bodies, it also harms our world.

As far back as the 1200s, people have been concerned about the quality of the air on Earth. After all, we only have one planet and one atmosphere.

The atmosphere is made up of the gases that surround Earth. It has many layers. The layer closest to Earth's surface, the troposphere, is very dense. It is only about 10 miles (16 kilometers) thick. Most of our weather happens in the troposphere because most of the water vapor is found there. Water vapor is important for making rain and clouds. The main gas in the atmosphere is nitrogen. Nitrogen makes up about 78 percent of the atmosphere, oxygen makes up 21 percent, about 1 percent is argon, and a small percentage is made up of various other gases. All of these gases exist in a careful, balanced state. If there was too much oxygen, everything would become more flammable. If there wasn't enough, nothing would burn, and we would not be able to breathe. The makeup of the atmosphere is important.

Particle Pollution

As you can see, it is important that we keep the air clean and balanced. If the wrong gases enter the atmosphere, they can cause serious problems for our environment and the health of all living things. There are multiple types of pollution that affect the air around us. One of the most common types of air pollution is particulate matter. Sometimes this is called "particle pollution." Particulate matter is made up of very tiny bits of material and liquid that get mixed into the air. Ash, dust, lead, soot, and smoke are all examples of particulate matter. Sometimes you can see the matter. Sometimes you can't.

So where do all of these tiny particles come from? One place we find particulate matter is a car's exhaust pipe. It can also be produced at a construction site, on an unpaved road, or from a large fire. Some particulate matter forms in the atmosphere when powerful chemicals react to each other. These chemicals are often released from power plants and other factories. Why does particulate matter, matter? For one thing, it can have major adverse effects on physical health. Because we breathe in particulate matter, it can get deep into our lungs and bloodstreams. Studies have linked particulate matter to asthma, lung irritation, irregular heartbeat, and even heart attacks. When it comes to the environment, fine particles are the main cause of haze in the United States. If you've ever driven through a congested city and experienced

All day long, pollution escapes from exhaust pipes on cars.

low visibility—a hazy cloudiness that is hard to see through—you were probably seeing a buildup of particulate matter in the air. Particulate matter, when carried through the air and deposited in the ground and water, can have harmful effects on coastlines, river basins, forests, and farms.

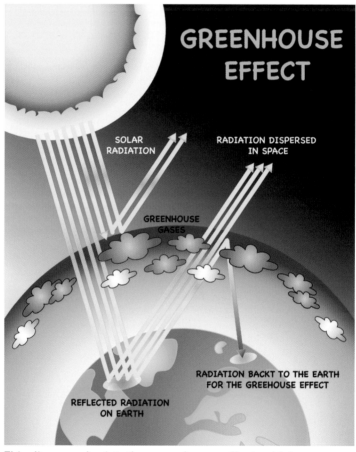

GREENHOUSE EFFECT

SOLAR RADIATION

RADIATION DISPERSED IN SPACE

GREENHOUSE GASES

RADIATION BACKT TO THE EARTH FOR THE GREEHOUSE EFFECT

REFLECTED RADIATION ON EARTH

This diagram depicts the greenhouse effect, which contributes to global warming.

It's a Gas

Particulate matter isn't the only type of harmful pollution. Today, one of the most disturbing types of air pollution occurs when substances mix with air in the atmosphere. This happens when fossil fuels burn. A fossil fuel is a substance like gas or coal that produces energy when it is burned. Believe it or not, fossil fuels are created from the remains of living organisms. Over thousands of years and tons of compression underground, materials like oil, coal, and gas are created. We extract them from the ground and burn them. The burning of fossil fuels happens in power plants and factories, and in vehicles whenever they are driven. The activity of burning these fuels

/ DID YOU KNOW? /

Global emissions reports show that China, with its large size, industrial focus, and lack of preventative policies, is the world's leading emitter of carbon dioxide. Don't get too excited, though—the United States comes in at number two. The European Union, Russia, and Japan round out the top five biggest emitters of greenhouse gases.

Technically, the smoke and ash that escape from a volcano can be considered air pollution.

adds carbon dioxide into the atmosphere. Carbon dioxide, or CO_2, is a colorless gas. You cannot see it. However, its presence does not go unnoticed. All of that CO_2 absorbs heat that radiates from Earth and keeps it trapped within our atmosphere. Because the heat enters the atmosphere and then stays inside, carbon dioxide and other gases like it are often called greenhouse gases.

On its own, carbon dioxide is not a toxic pollutant. We encounter it in soft drinks, dry ice, and even in fire extinguishers. When we exhale, a tiny bit of CO_2 leaves our lungs. But when we burn fossil fuels and allow huge amounts of CO_2 into the air, the greenhouse effect takes place. The greenhouse effect

IS AIR POLLUTION "NATURAL?"

While there are many clear sources of air pollution caused by humans, you may come across people or sources that point to "natural" air pollution. This might sound crazy, but it's true! Think of the ash that sprays out of volcanoes, the dust created in the desert, or fires that start naturally in forests and on grasslands. All of these events put gases and particulate matter into the atmosphere.

Some people even consider animals in their natural habitats as contributors to air pollution. Animals and people create pollution through methane production (gas!) and other bodily processes. It's important to remember that human activities and technologies are the main sources of poor air quality in our world today, but natural sources play a role too.

means that the atmosphere traps carbon dioxide and other harmful chemicals burned by fossil fuels. Like a greenhouse, the trapped substances lead to increased temperatures. An increase in Earth's temperature can lead to changes in climate and weather patterns, called global warming.

Many environmental scientists believe strongly that the greenhouse effect is a major cause of climate change. We see the effects of climate change almost every day as our weather patterns become more and more extreme. We experience warmer weather and major weather disasters such as hurricanes, wildfires, floods, and tropical storms, among other things. Additionally, the warming of Earth means that the planet's ice caps have begun to melt—and this process is only speeding up. As the ice caps melt, the melted water makes sea levels rise. All of these changes have an affect on animal habitats, plants, entire ecosystems, and even towns and countries.

Of course, not all CO_2 emissions remain in the atmosphere. Carbon dioxide is absorbed by the oceans as well as by plants. These are often called "carbon sinks." These "sinks" can help reduce the amount of warming Earth experiences. You might hear scientists refer to "plant sinks" or "ocean sinks." However, we can't rely on the oceans and plants to absorb all of the CO_2 we put into the air when we drive cars and burn fuel. In order to prevent the planet from warming to very dangerous levels, we need to decrease energy use, explore other, more renewable and Earth-friendly (or "green") energy forms, and research other solutions. Our air desperately needs us to make some changes, not only for our future health, but for our planet's safety and life's continued existence on Earth. The work has only just begun.

/ DID YOU KNOW? /

Carbon monoxide is a pollutant that can be found indoors. It can be produced from a grill, gas stove, fireplace, car engine, furnace, and more. It is colorless and odorless and, unlike greenhouse gases, which build up over a long period of time in the atmosphere, carbon monoxide can quickly turn interior air from breathable to deadly. You should make sure you have a carbon monoxide detector in your home!

CHAPTER TWO

AIR POLLUTION TODAY

A ir pollution is not a new problem. If you look back in history, there is evidence that humans caused significant air pollution over five thousand years ago! These first incidents of pollution resulted from the manufacture of tools and coins in smelters. Since the beginning, humanity's desire to make objects has tainted Earth's air supply.

Research done by archaeologists and scientists has helped us understand the story of early air pollution.

Opposite: Today, a huge percentage of air pollution comes from industrial activity—factories, power plants, and more.

During the twentieth and twenty-first centuries, archaeologists dug for copper coins and tools near the Dead Sea, while scientists extracted ice cores from Greenland that showed copper deposits. Their findings resulted in an explanation that the wind carried metal particles through the air all the way from the Mediterranean Sea to Greenland. Remember, this was manufacturing at its most primitive. If the air was affected by the earliest attempts at creation, just imagine what effect new, more plentiful and harmful substances have on the atmosphere in the twenty-first century!

Today, we manufacture goods at hyper-speed, almost always growing our manufacturing power in order to keep up with demand. This constant growth has been the norm since the Industrial Revolution. This period lasted from about the mid-1700s to the mid-1800s, and is marked for the sudden growth of industry—making and selling things. During this time, new machines were built, new processes were created, and the production of goods became more efficient. From the start of the Industrial Revolution until well into the nineteenth and twentieth centuries, air pollution in major European and US cities grew exponentially. During these years, walking through London was like walking through a cloud of smog. But people didn't really mind. In fact, many cities were proud of their smoggy air, since it made them feel as though they were advancing economically and socially.

As the years passed, the air grew worse. In 1893, Chicago hosted the World's Fair, a huge exposition for technological advancements. The centerpiece was a group of buildings known as the White City. However,

The 1893 World's Fair was tainted by thick, gray smog.

A woman and her children wear face masks outside to protect themselves from air pollution in New Delhi, India.

due to the heavily polluted air, the White City didn't stay white for long. Even before the fair opened, the area was covered in greasy soot and ash.

After that, residents of the world's most polluted cities began to question how much they really enjoyed living in smog-filled urban areas. Very, very slowly, some businesses and cities began to move toward a vision of cleaner air.

Today, cities in the United States and Europe aren't nearly as smoggy as they once were. While there are still low-visibility days and dangerous particulates in the air, the situation has improved. Other countries, still in the process of developing their industrial infrastructures, are dealing with the heavily clouded, smog-filled environments that Chicago, London, New York City, and other cities once experienced. In many large Asian cities, for instance, it is not uncommon for adults and children to wear masks to protect their lungs from the air pollution. Now that we know the adverse health effects of particulate matter, face masks are big business!

Even though we may not be able to see the pollution in the air all the time, it is still very present, especially at the atmospheric level. In the twenty-first century, more than ever before, we need to be aware of the ways in which air pollution has the potential to wreak havoc on the planet. If you watch the news, read weather reports, or go outside and note the changes in plants and bugs, you can see that global warming is happening. Greenhouse gases are a huge part of the problem.

We already know that increasing amounts of CO_2 in the atmosphere cause everything to heat up.

So why don't we just stop releasing it? As it turns out, the problem is much more complicated. There are other greenhouse gases in the air—water vapor, methane, nitrous oxide, and man-made chemicals. If we stopped all emissions of carbon dioxide today, the concentrations of greenhouse gases in the atmosphere would linger for centuries and wouldn't reach pre-Industrial Revolution levels for hundreds of years. Damage has already been done.

Whenever the greenhouse effect takes place, gases are not only trapped inside the atmosphere, but they absorb infrared radiation from the sun once they are there. This process helps heat up the earth. Carbon dioxide and methane are two of the main players in this game, but scientists are still discovering other greenhouse gases in the air. Two of these gases are nitrogen trifluoride and sulfuric fluoride. They are used to make flat-screen televisions and pest killers, respectively. These two gases, though they make up only a tiny portion of the atmosphere, are extremely potent and have the potential, if we continue producing them, to significantly contribute to global

Flat-screen televisions are made of nitrogen trifluoride, a potent greenhouse gas.

warming. However, we cannot isolate just one or two emissions and solve the problem. Greenhouse gases come from a variety of sources, and new ones are being discovered each year.

Where Do the Gases Come From?

Historically, manufacturing has been a major source of air pollution. Harmful gases, such as nitrogen trifluoride, sulfuric fluoride, CO_2, and sulfur dioxide, are created when certain materials are heated to high temperatures in factories. Since the chemicals released

How many household appliances do you use each day?
How much electricity does your daily routine require?

by this burning cannot stay inside the buildings, they are released into the atmosphere.

However, greenhouse gases aren't just created directly from the making of objects. Manufacturing also uses extremely large amounts of electricity to create items, put them together, and package them. Electricity is usually generated by the burning of coal, diesel fuel, or natural gas. That burning process releases greenhouse gases into the atmosphere. Think about it: How much electricity do you use throughout the day? When you charge your phone, cook food in the microwave, turn on the television, or even use water that has been heated up, you are using electricity! It is easy to point to manufacturing as a major climate change culprit, but whenever we use electricity that comes from one of these sources, we are contributing to global warming.

Another major source of carbon dioxide and other greenhouse gases is transportation. Trains, trucks, ships, and airplanes all help get things where they need to go. However, in order to move, they burn fuel. When vehicles burn fuel, just like a factory or

/ DID YOU KNOW? /

When you think of air pollution, you probably think of local sources—the factories, cars, and other things around you that cause the air in your community to be polluted. But the air doesn't recognize borders. Pollution often flows freely between the United States, Mexico, and Canada, as well as between North America and other continents. Researchers continue to study the unique circumstances surrounding transboundary air pollution and consider what policies we can put in place to protect our neighbors' air as well as our own.

power plant, they release carbon dioxide into the air. It doesn't matter if the vehicle is a car full of gasoline or a truck that runs on diesel. They are both fossil fuels that are released into the air as exhaust. You can see exhaust as it spews out the back of cars on the road. It comes out of an exhaust pipe and looks like smoke. Exhaust is made up of nitrogen, water, carbon dioxide, carbon monoxide, soot, and more. Carbon monoxide can be deadly—this is why you don't run a car for a long time inside a small, enclosed space. Carbon dioxide is a greenhouse gas. And soot is just stinky, messy, and bad for our lungs!

When one car drives down the road and lets exhaust out of its tailpipe, the harm to the atmosphere is minimal. However, when hundreds of millions of cars drive in countries around the world each day, the fumes add up. We can see this visually in cities with large populations. Many cars are packed into a small space, such as Los Angeles, California, or Delhi, India. The larger the car, the more exhaust it produces, and over the years, cars have only become larger. An SUV or Hummer contributes far more CO_2 to the air than a midsize sedan or compact car. Semi trucks, which

Tractor-trailers that haul goods across the country burn gallons of fossil fuels and release pollution into the air.

transport goods and travel back and forth across the country day after day, are some of the worst producers of all. Once they reach their destinations, some of those semis are emptied and their goods are moved to airplanes, or their containers are put directly onto ships. Due to a rapid increase in globalization, we are seeing a rise in this type of transportation. International trade has imports (items coming into a country) and exports (items going out) always on the move. This means that more and more ships and airplanes are traveling back and forth between various countries, burning more fuel.

Energy Options

OK, so the burning of fossil fuels contributes to global warming and climate change. Aren't we living in the twenty-first century? What about nuclear power? What about "clean coal?"

Nuclear

While renewable energy sources like solar and wind have gained traction across North America in recent years, nuclear power remains a huge source of energy. Today, it accounts for more than 30 percent of all energy produced in the United States. Canada relies on the energy source somewhat less, using nuclear power for about 16 percent of total electricity. Mexico, with only two nuclear reactors, relies on nuclear for almost 4 percent of its electricity. Across the United States, there are ninety-nine nuclear reactors. Six US states count nuclear power as their main source of electricity. Several new power plants are expected to be built by 2020.

Nuclear facilities like this one are an option when it comes to generating energy.

Over the course of the United States' history, nuclear power has often been promoted as a safe, efficient, and clean alternative to the burning of coal and natural gas. However, since their start in the 1960s, nuclear power plants have been the cause of many major disasters around the world. These disasters not only harmed the health of people living in affected areas, but they released radioactive gases into the atmosphere. Accidents like these, as well as concerns about radioactive waste disposal, have slowed the nuclear industry in recent years.

Some environmentalists have pushed for nuclear power as a form of "clean" energy, but it isn't entirely free from greenhouse gas emissions. In order to mine, extract, transport, and refine the element uranium, which is used in nuclear power plants, we still need to burn fossil fuels. Fossil fuels are used to build the reactors, process the waste that is produced, and transport that waste. Some reports state that nuclear power produces nearly one-third of the emissions from traditional coal-fired plants. That number is not insignificant. In the coming years, it will be up to us to decide which types of power we want to invest in and which to wean ourselves from. Before we commit to a "clean" form of energy, it's important to make sure that the production of that energy won't contribute to global warming.

Coal

As the United States' cheapest and most abundant source of energy, coal is ever present in the lives of Americans. About one-third of the country's energy is generated through the burning of coal. Countless jobs are connected to the coal industry. Reserves in

EVIDENCE OF OLD PROBLEMS FOUND IN OLD LUNGS

In 2011, researchers working at the KNH Centre for Biomedical Egyptology at the University of Manchester in England found evidence of pollution in the lungs of Egyptian mummies. Particulate matter, not unlike the tiny particles that irritate our lungs today, was found in these mummies that lived thousands of years ago. Some of the mummies were everyday workers, while others were members of the upper class, living as noblemen, priests, and priestesses. Ancient Egypt was preindustrial, without the cars and factories we have today. However, people did engage in cooking, mining, and metalworking, which generate air pollution. They probably also inhaled tiny particulates from their natural desert environment. Researchers continue to dig deeper into the causes of particulate matter in the lungs of mummies. Someday soon, we may know even more.

the United States are so abundant that they could burn coal at present rates for the next 275 years. Unfortunately, coal power is one of the most polluting and dangerous forms of energy production. Each year, coal-fired power plants cause asthma attacks, heart attacks, and "black lung," a deadly, painful condition that occurs in longtime coal miners. In addition to adverse health effects, the burning of coal pumps carbon dioxide into the atmosphere, contributing to global warming in a huge way.

Coal plants also produce acid rain. When fossil fuels are burned, sulfur dioxide and nitrogen oxide are released into the air. Then, these chemicals combine with water in the atmosphere. They fall as acid rain, or rain that is filled with acidic chemicals. This is a type of both air pollution and water pollution. The chemicals begin their polluting journey as emissions into the air, and end up in our water. Acid rain falls onto forests, farms, and other natural spaces that need to be kept clean from harmful chemicals. It soaks into the ground, plants, and waterways. Sometimes, it kills plants by eating away at natural protective coatings on leaves. It can kill fish and cause illness in animals

Coal is cut from underground mines. Workers wear protective gear and masks to help keep the dirty air out of their lungs.

that drink from affected lakes and rivers. Then, if people rely on that same water and those animals for food and drink sources—you can only imagine the cycle of harm that can be caused by acid rain. This cycle can only be prevented if we refrain from burning fossil fuels, or find a cleaner way.

Natural Gas

Another cheap and abundant form of power in today's world is natural gas. When people talk about natural gas, they are not referring to gasoline, which

WHEN IN ROME

While the ancient Egyptians have given us clues into some of the earliest types of air pollution, it was the Romans who were the first to take up the issue as a public problem that might necessitate a solution. Ancient Romans kept domesticated livestock, such as cows, sheep, and goats, that produced large amounts of methane. They also practiced blacksmithing, which could only be done using hot, ever-burning fires that also produced methane. Over time, Roman citizens complained about their dense city and its smoke pollution from blacksmiths, cooking, and eventually the smelting that produces lead and copper. Some Romans took their complaints to court, filing formal cases about the smoke problem. In 535, Emperor Justinian wrote about the importance of clean air,

"By the law of nature these things are common to mankind—the air, running water, the sea." But the Romans' attempts to stop the smoke creation and air pollution would go unheeded as the years passed, and the Industrial Revolution eventually tipped the scales toward ever more emissions.

The greenhouse gases and smoke created from blacksmithing plagued ancient Roman cities.

In the twenty-first century, natural gas storage facilities dot the American landscape.

is made from oil. Natural gas is a mixture. It contains methane and small amounts of ethane, propane, butane, pentane, and other substances. Just like coal and oil, natural gas forms when decomposing plant and animal matter is heated and squished between Earth's layers for millions of years. All of those plants had obtained energy from the sun. That energy remains trapped within the natural gas. When we light it, we get energy that we can use for generating electricity, cooking on a gas stove, or heating our homes. Some vehicles even run off of natural gas.

The word "natural" might cause us to believe that natural gas is clean and doesn't emit any dangerous chemicals, but that isn't true. In fact, the burning of natural gas, as well as the processing of gas that turns it from raw fuel into a marketable product, produce hydrocarbons, carbon dioxide, helium, and more. These emissions contribute to the greenhouse effect. Additionally, since natural gas is composed of methane, it is actually a bigger contributor to the greenhouse effect, because methane is more efficient at trapping heat than carbon dioxide. Researchers and scientists are split on which is worse for the atmosphere: coal or natural gas. Both put harmful chemicals into the air. Unlike coal, natural gas has the tendency to leak out into the atmosphere during its extraction and transportation. It is commonly extracted using a process called fracking, which utilizes water in order to take the natural gas out of its deeply dug wells.

Where Do We Go from Here?

By now, it is clear the greatest impact on air pollution is the creation and use of energy. When we create energy—be it through mining and burning coal, using fracking to extract and burn natural gas, drilling for and burning gasoline, building and maintaining nuclear reactors, or otherwise—we are contributing to global warming and climate change through the emission of dangerous gases into the atmosphere. When we use that energy to power vehicles, run factories, manufacture objects, heat homes, or cook food, we continue to release gases into the air. Is this it? Are we doomed to repeat these cycles

An oil well is designed to bring petroleum oil and hydrocarbons up from deep below Earth's surface.

over and over until all fossil fuels are gone and we have used up every ounce of energy we have left, poisoning the atmosphere and cooking the planet in the process? Or are there alternative forms of energy and other options?

As we will see, researchers, scientists, business leaders, and policymakers are coming up with new solutions every day. If we want to breathe clean air and power our complex lives, we will have to remain innovative and dedicated. If we do that, we may be able, eventually, to breathe some deep sighs of relief.

/ DID YOU KNOW? /

The United States Environmental Protection Agency (EPA) is a federal government agency. It works to protect human and environmental health by writing and enforcing regulations, giving grants to programs and educational institutions, studying environmental issues, and sponsoring partnerships. The EPA was established in 1970 under President Richard Nixon. The head of the EPA is appointed by the president, and the agency is headquartered in Washington, DC.

CHAPTER THREE

MODERN SOLUTIONS AND INNOVATORS

Remember that deep breath you took earlier? How your lungs expanded and you could feel the air rush out of your chest, nose, and mouth? That is a beautiful, universal feeling that each and every person deserves to experience thousands of times a day. There must be ways we can work together to protect clean air and ease of breathing, one of our most basic human rights. No child or adult deserves to live with asthma, or to wear a face mask whenever

Opposite: Tall, graceful wind turbines are one "clean" option for producing electricity.

Air pollution is truly a global problem. In fact, in 2016, the World Health Organization released data showing that 92 percent of the world's population lives in places where air pollution exceeds safe limits.

they go outside, or to squint into smog while they drive along the highway. Our world shouldn't live this way either—plagued by particulates and an excess of greenhouse gases, warming to ever higher temperatures. If we are going to make changes and reverse even a small percentage of the damage that has already been done, we have to look for creative strategies and innovative solutions. It is not enough to simply "cut back" on fossil fuels or continue with the policies we have. We need big changes, and we need them soon.

Clean (or Clean-er) Energy

You've probably heard the phrase "clean energy" before. In newspapers, on television, and on the lips of everyone these days are the buzzwords that may or may not help us kick our addiction to dirty fossil fuels. "Clean energy" can be used to describe two different things: renewable sources of energy that don't create as much pollution, and nonrenewable sources of energy that have reduced impacts on human health and the environment. We'll start with solutions that build on our current, nonrenewable energy sources, "clean" coal and natural gas.

As we've learned, coal is one of the cheapest and most abundant sources of energy in the United States, but its combustion is also a major cause of air pollution. Acid rain, health problems, and greenhouse gases all plague the coal industry. In the last few years, companies and interest groups have championed the idea of clean coal technology as a solution to our air pollution woes. The phrase entered the general lexicon around 2008, when the coal industry began using it heavily in advertising. There are several different strategies out there for "cleaning" coal, but at its most basic, the term refers to the process of capturing the carbon dioxide that is emitted from smokestacks when coal is burned. Then, the CO_2 could be injected into the ground and buried, hopefully keeping it from entering the atmosphere. This type of technology is also known as carbon capture and storage, or CCS.

While CCS is a very new technology, the federal government is currently subsidizing the coal industry's efforts to further develop and expand it. Today, there is only one coal plant in the United States that is using CCS. Affordable, efficient CCS technology is still years away, and the process does have its vocal critics. Many people are concerned that Earth does not have the capacity to store all of the carbon produced, limiting

This carbon capture plant is located in the Sahara desert near In Salah, Algeria.

the use of CCS. Others have serious concerns about the effects of carbon sequestration on our natural underground water sources and soil. Once all that CO_2 is buried underground, we aren't 100 percent sure what effects it will have on Earth. To many scientists, this sounds like a risky move, no matter how much CO_2 it keeps out of the atmosphere!

The phrase "clean coal" can also refer to highly efficient coal plants that emit somewhat less CO_2 into the atmosphere than older plants. These new plants do not use carbon capture, but they remain expensive, so it is unlikely that we will see those technologies expand much further.

Carbon capture and sequestration techniques aren't limited to coal plants. These solutions have also been tried at natural gas power plants. Since the year 2000, the production of shale gas in the United States has expanded exponentially, driving down the prices of natural gas and sending the industry into a tailspin of profits. Fracturing, more commonly known as "fracking," has expanded across the country, and many in the industry would like to see CCS become a regular part of the fracking process.

Renewable Energy

Even though coal and natural gas are the most popular forms of energy production in the United States, they are not our only options. Solar and wind energies have become more and more popular as business owners, scientists, and families all become more aware of the need for renewable energy sources. Sometimes these options are called "alternative energy sources," because they are technically alternatives to coal and gas. But it is possible for them to become mainstream sources if enough people get on board! In fact, some states now let individuals choose the source of their

Rooftop solar panels can help homeowners reduce their carbon footprint.

electricity. You could choose all fossil fuels. You could have some of your electricity come from wind and solar. You could even choose to have 100 percent of the electricity in your home come from renewable energy sources like wind and solar panels! This is not uncommon, and as the technology becomes more efficient and advanced, the energy itself goes down in price. Today, more than ever before, it is possible to power your home using energy that does not produce air pollution or contribute to global warming.

Wind

Wind energy is one of the simplest (and some would argue most beautiful) forms of energy generation we have on the market today. Wind turbines, which you may have seen dotting a flat field or even out at sea, hugging a coastline, convert the kinetic energy inside wind into mechanical power. The blades of a wind turbine are turned by the wind itself, which powers an electric generator that supplies an electric current. You can think of it as the opposite of a fan. A turbine uses wind to make electricity—and it does it without creating particulate matter or putting CO_2 and other harmful chemicals into the atmosphere. It is also renewable. No matter how much wind we use, there will always be more wind. We cannot use it up.

Since 2008, the cost of wind power has decreased dramatically. The most expensive part of building a wind farm is the machinery itself. Turbines are extremely tall and heavy machines. Critics also cite the inconvenience of wind farms. They are often located in remote areas, far from the big cities in need of electric power. One of the biggest issues with wind energy is its reliability—if it isn't a windy day, no power is generated. Unlike coal or natural gas, the supply isn't always around and waiting to be dug out of the ground. Wind farms rely on the weather. Slowly but surely, this form of clean, sustainable energy is becoming more popular in the United States and abroad.

Solar and Hydropower

Another form of renewable energy that has been gaining popularity in the twenty-first century is solar power. Unlike wind turbines, which have to be installed in large farm-like venues, solar panels can be used in both large- and small-scale models. Many families have solar panels installed on their homes for personal use, providing clean electricity and heat. There are a few different types of solar power generation, but at its most basic, solar power involves the conversion of sunlight into energy. Sometimes this happens directly—sunlight is converted into an electric current using photovoltaic cell technology. Some solar plants use a solar thermal energy process, which uses the solar energy to make steam. The steam is then turned into electricity through a turbine. Like wind, solar energy is renewable. The sun is always in the sky, and solar power generation even happens on cloudy days. Solar cells remain relatively expensive to install on one's home, so they have not taken off in the United States. However, as with most alternative energies, the price continues to fall little by little, and those in the industry predict that we will see more solar as we move into the 2020s.

Solar and wind aren't the only forms of renewable energy, of course. Hydropower, harnessing the energy created by water; geothermal, energy derived from the heat produced naturally inside Earth; and biomass, the use of waste and agricultural products to create energy, round out the top five most commonly used renewable energy sources. Though all of these sources continue to gain popularity, none of them have the market share that coal and natural gas still have in the United States. So, until renewable resources become the norm, we will have to search for other innovations to help us reduce air pollution and greenhouse gas emissions.

Transportation Solutions

Electricity generation isn't the only source of air pollution that is adding to global warming and climate change. In the United States as well as across the

Cars continue to produce pollution even after they are disposed of in a junk yard.

globe, one of the largest sources of air pollution is also an old pastime, a huge industry, and a daily task for many: driving. Today, more than one billion vehicles are out on the road across the planet. That number continues to grow each year. However, our reliance on cars, trucks, and motorcycles is costly. Every part of the process—from a car's creation, to its time on the road, to its eventual demise—contributes to harmful air pollution and global warming. A car's body, usually made of steel, glass, rubber, and plastic, demands tons of processing of raw materials. These materials first need to be removed from the earth through mining or drilling. Then they are heated, shaped, and constructed. According to researchers, the process of making one new car from raw materials can produce almost 40 tons (36 metric tons) of carbon dioxide. Before the car is even on the road, it will have produced half of all the air pollution it will create in its lifetime! Another 7 percent of a car's lifetime pollution comes from its disposal, after it has had a life of driving. However, 80 percent of a car is recyclable. If we made a habit of recycling our vehicles when we were finished with them, humans could save a significant amount of air pollution from entering the atmosphere.

Aside from owning our cars longer and simply driving less, there are other, more innovative and game-changing solutions being explored in the automobile industry today. As people learn more about climate change, they have started to demand cars that pollute less. All of that demand has led the major car companies to invest in research and development of "cleaner" cars. Sometimes this just means creating very fuel-efficient vehicles that are still powered by gasoline. Other new advancements are hybrid vehicles, which are powered in part by electricity. The Toyota Prius and Honda Insight are popular hybrid brands that use this technology and also have increased gas mileage. As you drive a hybrid vehicle, the electric battery recharges itself, though the car still relies on a traditional engine and gasoline.

The next step beyond a hybrid car is a fully electric vehicle. These are in development, and many are already on the market, by several major car companies and even some newer players in the industry. The Nissan LEAF, Chevrolet Bolt EV, and Kia Soul EV are just a few examples of the electric options on the market for the everyday user, while Volvo, Audi, BMW, and other luxury brands are also producing electric and hybrid cars. Tesla Inc. recently disrupted the industry by introducing the first mass-produced all-electric sports car, the Model 3, in 2017. Since revealing its first car, the Roadster, in 2008, Tesla has put the Model X, an electric luxury SUV, on the market, as well as the Model S, a more affordable sedan, in addition to offering its own solar panels for home installation and use. The Tesla brand has become extremely popular very quickly, a milestone in the electric car and renewable energy markets.

In the United States, as well as in China and other countries, the government continues to offer subsidies and incentives both for automakers and consumers. These efforts are an attempt to build the electric vehicle industry and move away from traditional combustion engines that spew pollution into the air.

Another innovation that has yet to take off but is an option in the auto market is a car powered by hydrogen fuel cells. Fuel cells produce electricity through chemical reactions. They rely on hydrogen, which can be derived from natural gas or even from water, though energy is required to break apart the water molecules. Fuel cells are silent, long lasting, and have extremely low emissions. However, currently, the United States does not have the infrastructure needed to support hydrogen fuel cell cars, such as hydrogen refueling stations and the equipment needed to supply those stations. The US system is set up to support traditional, internal-combustion vehicles that rely on gasoline. Gradually, the industries are taking steps to move away from that system and onto a path toward cleaner, less-polluting vehicles. Perhaps hydrogen-powered cars will be more common in the future.

Electric cars, like this Smart Fortwo, are becoming more popular, especially in urban communities.

Policies and Agreements

Of course, changes in transportation can't be driven by the industries alone. In the early twenty-first century, the US government and other countries around the world have committed to making positive changes in emissions policies. One of the main sources of policy on air pollution and climate change in the United States is the Environmental Protection Agency (EPA). This government agency sets emissions and fuel economy standards for the country's cars, trucks, planes, and more. These regulations set greenhouse gas standards for different vehicles, forcing the industries to change the ways in which they produce their vehicles. Other such agencies and policies are in effect in other parts of the world too.

Many important technological and environmental innovations have been pursued by companies that are largely reacting to consumer demand. However, outside of that system, governments have also been working hard to reduce air pollution and greenhouse gas emissions through policies and laws. These strategies aren't new; the US government has been acting to reduce pollution through policy measures since the 1950s. In 1955, Congress passed the Air Pollution Control Act, authorizing research on air pollution. Five years later, Congress authorized research specifically on air pollution caused by automobiles.

The year 1963 marked the passing of the first Clean Air Act. The act established air quality standards based on research. By 1968, the act authorized emission standards for new motor vehicles. Further

/ DID YOU KNOW? /

You may have heard that lead can cause major health problems when it is found in our water, but did you know it can also pollute the air? Luckily, thanks to government regulations, EPA emissions controls, and the permanent phase-out of leaded gasoline, the United States decreased its airborne lead concentrations 98 percent between 1980 and 2005. Year after year, lead emissions continue to decrease. This is a positive change for the atmosphere, as well as the health of everyone on the planet.

amendments were made over the course of the next several decades to address state regulations, acid rain, ozone depletion, and gasoline formulations. The 1990 version of the Clean Air Act was the first to propose emissions trading to combat acid rain, a practice more commonly known as "cap and trade."

Emissions trading is an innovative policy measure that has gained traction over the last twenty years. The cap and trade approach utilizes the market to help control pollution. Essentially, it puts a "price" on carbon emissions. The process puts a "cap," or limit, on emissions and then creates permits. Companies, governments, and other entities hold one permit for every unit of pollution they emit. Then the organizations can buy and sell, trading the permits and, essentially, the share of pollution. This system puts a limit on pollution while giving businesses and countries the opportunity to choose how to stay within those limits. Ideally, the limits are lowered each year and the market adjusts accordingly. Additionally, the federal government receives income from the taxation of revenue earned from the trading of credits.

Another piece of the cap and trade system is the availability of carbon offsets. When heavy emitters of greenhouse gases—such as companies in the United States, China, and India—need to keep producing pollution at their current rates, they can invest in carbon reduction projects in the developing world. These investments "offset" the carbon produced by the companies. Both emissions trading and carbon offset programs have their champions and critics. Supporters are hopeful that market forces will ultimately lead to less air pollution and emissions. Detractors consider these programs a distraction and, ultimately, a socially unjust and ineffective attempt to reduce global emissions. As time goes on, we will see just how effective these policies might be.

In addition to market-based policy efforts, there have also been several international agreements on climate action and air pollution. As early as 1992, the United Nations adopted the Framework Convention on Climate Change (UNFCCC), a treaty that set nonbinding limits on greenhouse gas emissions and set up no mechanisms for enforcement. Since that time, other treaties within the UNFCCC have sought

Chinese cities like Harbin, pictured here, are some of the heaviest emitters of air pollution and greenhouse gases.

to set binding terms on countries, such as the Kyoto Protocol, which set targets for some (but not all) signing countries. Most recently, the Paris Climate Agreement, introduced in 2015, aimed to limit the global temperature increase. As of 2018, 174 countries had signed the accord. This is good news, as it shows a global effort to combat climate change and help protect the air around us.

Global Innovations

Government policies and alternative energy solutions aren't the only things that will help us achieve a

Biking is a popular "green" alternative to driving a fuel-burning vehicle.

world with clean air. Around the globe, researchers, scientists, and inventors are creating new and interesting ways to combat air pollution. Some of them are small-scale, affecting the particulate matter in a community or city center. Others are large-scale, with dreams of changing the habits of entire regions. These innovators are the people who will inspire technological breakthroughs and hopefully help to change the course of environmental history.

India

Long known as one of the densest and most polluted countries, India is taking huge steps to clean up the country's air. Energy minister Piyush Goyal is leading

FUNDING SOLUTIONS WHERE FUNDS ARE SCARCE

Did you know that pigeons are being used to fight air pollution? In London, England, Plume Labs has outfitted pigeons with wearable technology containing pollution sensors. These tiny backpacks monitor levels of ozone nitrogen dioxide and volatile compounds. The data is sent to a central hub and put up on the internet for Londoners to access through an easy-to-use map. Everyone can access the information on a web browser, mobile app, or through regular updates on Twitter. Runners, cyclists, and walkers can also join the Air Patrol by signing up to wear the devices themselves.

The Plume sensor fits comfortably on a pigeon's back.

the charge to transition India to 100 percent electric car usage by 2030. The federal government will back the efforts for the first few years by investing in charging infrastructure and battery swapping. After two or three years, government officials expect market demand to take over. Meanwhile, the country is also working to "go green" by expanding its solar capacity and renewing its commitment to the Paris Climate Agreement.

CityTree

One new startup is hoping to revolutionize the air quality in major cities. Green City Solutions, a company founded in Dresden, Germany, is seeing success with its CityTree, a mobile installation that removes pollutants from the air. Trees and other plants use their leaves to absorb pollution naturally. In Oslo, Norway; Paris, France; Brussels, Belgium; and Hong Kong, China; the CityTree is being used to do the same thing. But this isn't your average tree. The installation is a metal box 13 feet (4 m) tall, 9.8 feet (3 m) wide, and 7.2 feet (2.2 m) deep. Inside the box are moss cultures. The outside of the box has solar panels, and rainwater collects in a reservoir. There's even the option of having a bench connect to it. Wi-Fi sensors inside the installation help monitor the air quality and the effectiveness of the "tree." The company says the tree is as beneficial to an environment as planting 275 real trees. Today, about twenty CityTrees have been installed in cities across the world, fighting urban pollution every day. With a price tag of $25,000 though, the project may not be able to expand at a quick pace, especially in developing countries with elevated levels of air pollution.

Artistic Innovations

Even artists are getting in on efforts to curb air pollution. One such artist-turned-inventor, Daan Roosegaarde, has designed a bicycle that takes in polluted air as you ride it and then releases purified air in a cloud around the rider. Roosegaarde came up with the idea while he was living in Beijing. On weekdays, the city skyline is covered in smog. After designing the Smog Free Tower, a standalone structure that removes particulate matter from the air, he decided to apply the same technology to bicycles. Today, he is hoping that the smog-fighting bikes will be adopted by one of the popular bike-sharing programs in China. If used on a large scale, they could make a meaningful difference in the lives of urban dwellers in China and beyond.

Other innovators want to completely rethink the way we build our cities. Recently, Italian design firm Stefano Boeri Architetti unveiled plans for Liuzhou Forest City, a development to be built in southern China. The neighborhood, currently planned for 342 acres (138 hectares), would include over seventy buildings, both residential and commercial. Those buildings would then be covered with forty thousand trees and nearly one million other plants.

Ready to unplug? Paying attention to your electricity usage is one way you can help reduce air pollution.

The neighborhood could hold up to thirty thousand people—the size of a large town. The nature-focused design is expected to absorb almost 10,000 tons (9,071 metric tons) of carbon dioxide a year, produce 900 tons (816 metric tons) of oxygen, and naturally decrease the air temperature. Construction on the Liuzhou Forest City is set to begin in 2020.

What Can You Do?

Amongst all these new inventions, exciting ideas, hardline policies, and changing energy infrastructures, what can everyday citizens do to help reduce air pollution? As it turns out, there are all kinds of things you can do! Without kids, teens, and families caring about the state of our air, nothing will ever change. It might feel like an insurmountable task—after all, there are billions of cars on the road, countless factories pumping chemicals into the atmosphere, and the planet is getting warmer every day. But we need everyone to stand up for clean air and help make meaningful change.

There are simple things you can do every day when it comes to making clean air choices. Since automobiles are one of the leading causes of air pollution, especially in urban areas, you can simply choose to use your car less. Instead of getting a ride to school, hop on your bike. Take advantage of the school bus, subway, or other public transportation. When you have to ride in a car, try to gather as many people as possible and create a carpool. And when you're using a ride-sharing application, look for options that put multiple users into one vehicle. These efforts will save miles, burn less fuel, and put fewer harmful chemicals into the environment.

Another simple switch is changing from a gas-powered lawn mower to an electric mower. Did you know an hour of mowing the grass with a gas-powered mower pollutes the air as much as driving a car for 50 miles (81 km)? There are lawn mowers that run on electricity, and even old-fashioned push mowers that require nothing more than your muscles to make them run.

Of course, when switching to electric options, it's important to think about the source of your electricity. Does your household choose renewable fuels for its electric supply? If not, see if your state allows you the option to easily switch. Using renewable energy like wind or solar in your home is one simple way to reduce your carbon footprint. This phrase refers to the sum of all greenhouse gas emissions induced by your activities during a certain time frame. Online carbon footprint calculators measure your energy use at home, your transportation choices, and the amount of waste you produce. Put together, these things make up your carbon footprint. You can set tangible, achievable goals to reduce your footprint in small ways each day.

When thinking about the amount of air pollution you personally contribute to the air, you can't avoid energy use. What are some small ways you can use less electricity in your home? Some solutions are simple. For instance, you can use less hot water in your shower and washing machine. You can unplug your electronics when you're not using them, including chargers, microwaves, and the television. Turn off the lights when moving from room to room. And think about the temperature! Can you turn down the heat a little in the winter? Put an extra blanket on your bed? In the summer, can you utilize fans instead of the air conditioner? Can you open all the windows and let in some of that air you are working so hard to keep clean? Small steps like these, when multiplied by the population of our world, can have a huge effect on air pollution and greenhouse gas emissions.

Planting trees, recycling, and eating organic foods are other ways to reduce your environmental impact. To find more, search online. Try to find information on local, state, and federal government officials. Email them to let them know that you care about the quality of your air, and that preserving clean air is critical for the future of our planet. Just like the policymakers, researchers, scientists, inventors, artists, and everyone out there working on behalf of clean air, you too can make a difference! Then, each time you take a breath and feel the fresh air move through your lungs, you will know that you helped to make it happen and keep it clean. It's up to us to breathe deep and act fast. The future of our atmosphere, our planet, and our air depends on us.

SPECK

Indoor air pollution creates health problems for people all across the globe. Particulate matter is released into homes through heating, cleaning, cooking, and more. In order to combat the health risks associated with particulate matter in homes, the CREATE Lab at Carnegie Mellon University (CMU) Robotics Institute created Speck. This product empowers everyday citizens to improve the air. It is a small, affordable, easy-to-use air purity monitor. It takes just two steps to set up. It monitors the air through a Wi-Fi connection. CMU first tested the device through the Carnegie Library of Pittsburgh, giving people the chance to monitor their air at no cost. The project's mission is to provide immediate, continual, cost-free feedback to families about their air quality and what they can do to improve it.

acid rain Any form of precipitation with chemical components that cause environmental harm.

carbon capture and storage The process of capturing carbon dioxide from fossil fuel power plants and depositing it underground.

carbon dioxide A colorless, odorless gas that is naturally present in air and absorbed by plants in photosynthesis.

carbon footprint The amount of greenhouse gases produced by a particular person or group.

carbon offsets A reduction of carbon emissions in one place in order to compensate for emissions made elsewhere.

emissions trading After setting a cap on emissions, entities receive permits to produce an amount of pollution, which they can then trade with others.

globalization The development of an integrated global economy.

hybrid A vehicle that uses more than one form of energy to propel itself, most often a combination of internal combustion engine and electric motor.

particulate matter A mixture of tiny solid and liquid particles, many of which are hazardous when inhaled, suspending in the air.

potent The ability to produce great power or effect.

smog A fog or haze that is made heavier by smoke and chemical fumes.

FURTHER INFORMATION

Books

Ajmera, Maya, and Dominique Browning.
  Every Breath We Take: A Book About Air.
  Watertown, MA: Charlesbridge, 2016.

Amstutz, L.J. *How Can We Reduce
  Transportation Pollution?* Minneapolis, MN:
  Lerner Publishing, 2016.

Feinstein, Stephen. *Solving the Air Pollution
  Problem: What You Can Do.* Berkeley
  Heights, NJ: Enslow Publishers, Inc., 2011.

Higgins, Matthew. *The Air Out There: How
  Clean Is Clean?* Mankato, MN: Norwood
  House Press, 2012.

Hustad, Douglas. *How Can We Reduce
  Manufacturing Pollution?* Minneapolis, MN:
  Lerner Publishing, 2016.

Websites

Air Quality Index for Kids

https://www.airnow.gov/index.cfm?action=aqikids.
index

Here you can learn about the Air Quality
Index, discover how to lower your risk from air
pollution, and play fun games.

Energy Kids

https://www.eia.gov/kids/index.cfm

Sources of energy, the history of energy, and
tips for saving energy are all found on this
comprehensive site sponsored by the US Energy
Information Administration.

Kids Ecology Corps

http://www.kidsecologycorps.org/our-environment/
natural-cycles/air-pollution

Learn more about the steps kids can take
to decrease air pollution and help protect
our planet.

SELECTED BIBLIOGRAPHY

"Air Pollution: Current and Future Challenges."
Clean Air Act Overview. EPA.gov. https://
www.epa.gov/clean-air-act-overview/air-
pollution-current-and-future-challenges.

Ajmera, Maya, and Dominique Browning.
Every Breath We Take: A Book About Air.
Watertown, MA: Charlesbridge: 2016.

Amstutz, L.J. *How Can We Reduce
Transportation Pollution?* Minneapolis, MN:
Lerner Publishing Group, 2016.

Carmichael, L.E. *How Can We Reduce
Agricultural Pollution?* Minneapolis, MN:
Lerner Publishing, 2016.

Feinstein, Stephen. *Solving the Air Pollution
Problem: What You Can Do.* Berkeley
Heights, NJ: Enslow Publishers, Inc., 2011.

Giles, Chris. "This 'Tree' Has the Environmental
Benefits of a Forest." CNN, June 7, 2017.
http://www.cnn.com/style/article/citytree-
urban-pollution/index.html.

Harris, Richard. "Air Pollution: Bad for Health,
Good for Planet?" NPR, November 11, 2011.
http://www.npr.org/2011/11/11/142218650/
air-pollution-bad-for-health-but-good-for-
planet.

Higgins, Matthew. *The Air Out There: How
Clean Is Clean?* Mankato, MN: Norwood
House Press, 2012.

Hustad, Douglas. *How Can We Reduce
Manufacturing Pollution?* Minneapolis, MN:
Lerner Publishing, 2016.

Institute of Medicine (US). *Committee on the
Effect of Climate Change on Indoor Air
Quality and Public Health.* Climate Change,
the Indoor Environment, and Health.
Washington, DC: The National Academies
Press, 2011.

Jacobson, Mark Z. *Air Pollution and Global Warming: History, Science, and Solutions.* Cambridge, UK: Cambridge University Press, 2012.

Miller, Debra A. *Pollution.* Detroit, MI: Greenhaven Press, 2012.

Morrison, Jim. "Air Pollution Goes Back Way Further Than You Think" Smithsonian.com, January 11, 2016. http://www.smithsonianmag.com/science-nature/air-pollution-goes-back-way-further-you-think-180957716.

Pidcock, Roz. "Analysis: What global CO2 Emissions Mean for Climate Change Goals." CarbonBrief, November 15, 2016. https://www.carbonbrief.org/what-global-co2-emissions-2016-mean-climate-change.

Plumer, Brad. "What 'Clean Coal' Is—and Isn't." *New York Times*, August 23, 2017. https://www.nytimes.com/2017/08/23/

climate/what-clean-coal-is-and-isnt.
html?mcubz=0.

Sechrist, Darren. *Air Pollution*. Tarrytown, NY:
Marshall Cavendish Corporation, 2009.

Spice, Byron. "Carnegie Mellon Spinoff
Introduces Speck, a Personal, Wi-Fi-
connected Air Quality Monitor." Carnegie
Mellon University News, March 16, 2015.
https://www.cmu.edu/news/stories/
archives/2015/march/speck-air-quality-
monitor.html.

Stromburg, Joseph. "Air Pollution Has Been
a Problem Since the Days of Ancient
Rome" Smithsonian.com, February 2013.
http://www.smithsonianmag.com/history/
air-pollution-has-been-a-problem-since-the-
days-of-ancient-rome-3950678/?page=1.

Vallero, Daniel. *Fundamentals of Air Pollution*.
Cambridge, MA: Academic Press, 2014.

INDEX

ABOUT THE AUTHOR

Kaitlyn Duling believes in the power of words to change hearts, minds, and, ultimately, actions. An avid reader and writer who grew up in Illinois, she now resides in Pittsburgh, Pennsylvania. She knows that knowledge of the past is the key to our future, and wants to make sure that all children and families have access to high-quality information. She loves to learn about and advocate for a healthy, sustainable environment.